Through the Mirror

Poetry of the Lonely

W. Blaine Wheeler

For those who have suffered greatly
and lost much

1

I think I saw you once
        long ago
When the roads were long
And our hearts were empty.
You asked me to go with you
To see how long the roads were
And I said
        no.

Only now do I understand
What you meant
        long ago
When you asked me to go with you
To see how long the roads were
When our hearts were empty
And I said
        no.

2

I want now to seek strongly
        the fullness of that fragile flower;
So let me cut the shadow
        of my soul
        for the dreaming time
        has gone
        and the living time
        has come.

Weave well my precious days,
        you weavers of fate,
        and let there be no
        flaws in your warp
        for I have no more
        of this material to give.

And let me find someone
    who will seek with me
    and who understands how
    short the season of that flower is.

For the dreaming time has gone
And the living time has come.

        3

You have told me the story many times before,
        old grandfather
        of the teas;
    but I will listen again
    as you carefully pour
    the hot green fragrance
And slowly tell me of the morning long ago,
        old grandfather
        of the teas,
    when your last daughter
    was born and died
    as the heavens
Over Nagasaki disappeared and ashes rained
On your home and your wife and your baby,
        old grandfather
        of the teas.

        4

What have you shown me this November night,
    widow Helena,
    in your small apartment
    near where St. Margaret's Island
Splits the Danube between Buda and Pest?

The old and small carefully kept photos
      tell too much
      of another November
      when your Mihaly
Was youthfully alive
Among the deadly tanks
Crumbling the ochre bricks
Along the boulevards
Where I walked this afternoon.

5

My bed your fragrance
Reminds me of too few hours
And too many hopes.

6

Unhurt by the falling night
And safe from dew's harm
You sat there in the soft light

Alone with your mind
Mirroring now those hopes
Of yesterday while keeping

Separate today's deeds
Lying as ash about
Blackened grates surrounding

Dead wills for tomorrow
In the mortal confines
Of your idiot told tale.

7

Reaching for joy and security and peace,
    but the greatest of these is security
    even though Hecate's chiefest mortal
    enemy is known,
Is what the bastillian foes did;
No less than the valleyforgians dreamed.

Hoping for self and wealth and fame,
    even when knowing this dear

    reaching is right, is wrong
       unless of course there is something
In the wheel not yet turned to the great
Burning light lingering in and shining out.

8

As our days shorten and darken at our end,
       we each know
       the other remains
       holding the other
       as in our beginning
When our days were long and bright.

9

Too many things left
Undone in our hastened life
As we say farewell.

10

Walking again through disordered vistas
      keenly I saw
      dim shapes wheeling
      brightly with their freedoms.

Knowing never enough of these enchantments
      which always spell,
      I reached quickly
      as the cacophonous
Furies splayed ephemerally their wares.

Grasping the first vivid display
      as usually I do,
      sparks from lessons
      eons ancient-wise
Sounded broadly across my mind.

Discarding finally the sorrowful joy
      hopeful thoughts emerged
      urging me to forget
      what never remains
And to look within for permanency.

11

High on the rough trail to Spanjola
      where weeds grow over forgotten
      Turkish footprints,
I met and spoke with a flower
Named Dika.
Shyly she offered me an orange
Meant for one of her six or seven
      brothers and sisters.
I think now I understand
      why the hot sun in Herceg-Novi
      seemed so cool,
And why we suddenly understood
One another that afternoon
      though neither spoke
      the other's language.

12

Flowers pressing against my garden
Sending captive fragrances out
      for me to savor
Seem now to startle me.

Earlier my ignorance led me
To pick and attempt to keep
      those joy-giving
God-given arousers of life.

Now the urge to have is far
Less than the need to enjoy
      in airy freedom
Along lonely paths in my garden.

13

There can be no time
When great pain is not a part
Of the end of hope.

14

Evening. A repetition of others beyond numbering
Lingers
Holding promises not given by harsh day
To us who wait for kind days
When all will be well
And
We won't have to wait for evening
To forget.

15

One more dance with hope today,
      and I am tired
      of movements strange
With little comfort or intent;
But the dancers form patterns
Once again lovingly new.

16

The said the ship left late
Yesterday afternoon,
      but they did not know
      if my loved ones
Made it.
I know I did not board

freedom
As I heard the harbor sounds
Here in my lonely cell.

17

Searching for yes goes far beyond
      philosophers' affirmation of life
And
      teachers' instruction of purposes;
Yes, when all is no, is a cruel
Seductress
      distantly ephemeral.

18

The train stopped. Again.
Hissing steam and a
Few distant clunks
Were all to be heard.

Desolate plowed earth
And two small metal
Buildings greeted our
Wandering tired eyes.

Soon brisk commands
Were heard. Husky men
Began passing enormous
Mirrors under the train
      looking for
          freedom riders.

19

Nothing is greater
Than the final loss of you
Who loved me so long.

20

I heard you once again
    in my dreams
      of better times.
And once again you told me
How
All will come together
    with no bitter memories
    of these days.

21

Do not scream for I am deaf from
    hearing my own screams
As I struggle to find me
Amid countless denials
    here and there
    yesterday and today.

22

Joy moves cautiously through these
    doors barely opened
    from dark to dark
With little hope that our tangled
    path can ever
    be illuminated.

23

The young man seemed startled
      when told
By the judge that humid afternoon
That buying what he did
Was a serious offense
      in Tampico.

24

There are no level roads;
Only roads made level
      by torment and hope,
      by rage and prayer,
      by despair and faith.

25

To walk laughing with you
Only once again
Is now my only dream
Here in the hard confines
Of my endless memories
Of what had once been
When we were so much in love.

26

Remaining alone
Can never be the answer
For our loneliness.

27

Old gentlelady standing under the dripping awning
With your red and yellow flowered
      kerchief tied
      under your chin
And wearing men's high-topped work shoes
      plainly visible
      beneath your
      once cream colored
Long dress now missing a belt and two buttons,
You have counted the clutch of coins
In your little purse three times
      while looking
      through the window
      at the bright
Display of children's toys and things.

28

I am sorry, sir,
I am forced to repossess
Your house Christmas Eve.

29

Reaching for my hand and attempting to smile
    as she had
    for our decades
    together,
She told me the lab reported a terminal cancer
And that we would now have little time left together.

Her words slammed into me as nothing ever before
    as I tried
    to grasp
    this awful finality;
All the while hoping that there had been a mistake,
And longing to do anything to save her from this destiny.

I cannot understand what is happening here,
And I certainly cannot walk this road without her.

30

Acoma, Chickasaw, Creek, Seminole,
Natches, Nez Perce, Dakota, Ute,
Sauk, Apache, Comanche, Sioux,
Cheyenne, Pawnee, Choctaw, Cree,
Ottawa, Delaware, Shawnee, Kickapoo,
Fox, Passamaquoddy, Blackfeet,
Arapaho, Flathead, Squamesh, Kiowa,
Hupa, Paiute, Wintun, Klamath, Coos,
Chinook, Mandan, Omaha, Osage,
Wichita, Languna, Mohawk, Seneca,
Cayuga, Onondaga, Oneida, Zuni.

The Mayflower; et cetera.

31

Seeing you in pain
When I am unable to help
Is killing my soul.

32

In days younger and wonderfully free
When the palm trees sang to us
      of love
      and wisdom,
All we could want were days in the sun
With our dreams of girls and life by the sea.
Then I saw the long black handkerchief
And I remembered your smile with grief.

In days older and filled with gladness
When our children sang to us
      of school
      and friends,
All we could want were years in our homes
With our families together apart from sadness.

Then I saw the long back handkerchief
And I remembered your smile with grief.

In days broken and eager with fight
When our nation sang to us
      of strength
      and freedom,
All we could want were chances in our land
To enjoy and keep what was our right.

Then I saw the long black handkerchief
And I remembered your smile with grief.

In days recent and gorged with lies

When our friends sang to me
      of sorrow
      and you,
All I could want were armies of angels
With swords of fire to avenge your cries.

Then I would forget the long black handkerchief
And I would not remember your smile with grief.

                Benghazi
                April 1977
                for Mohammed Ali ben Amer

33

I walked downtown this morning
              with nothing more
            on my mind
Then going to Ike's Chili Parlor for a big bowl
To ward off the biting cold of a winter's day.
On my way
The sidewalk took me past
The Workers' Compensation and Unemployment Benefits building.
In front in a parked car were three people
            who knew exactly
            where they were.
The young wife was crying.
The little boy was screaming.
The thin husband was shouting.

34

When one of us must sit alone,
    as all must,
In a room with darkened memories;
What is the solace for the sorrowed one
    left alone?
Can reading those letters of long ago
    written in joyful times
Or remembering all of our together moments
Remove the relentless pain of a forever
    separation
Which steadily conquers the soul
    so completely?

35

No room for you here.

It is the season, you know.
Besides, you look poor.

36

Leukemia.
Feared word to all who would live.
I arrived too late
      to be with you;
Too late to tell you
      all the things
        I should have
      years ago.

37

I have seen you lying drunk in a dirty coat
      on the greens in Edinburgh;
Urinating boldly while people laughed
      in an alley in Chicago;
Begging for bread as crowds passed you
      in the square in Zadar;
Staring at jeans you will never have
      on foreigners in Bucharest;
And should I go someday to Moosejaw,
I suppose you would also be there.

38

Rubicon River crossed by the
      unnatural born man
Who would scorn the Ides
      sets the stage
For all roads leading to the
      seven-hilled City
Where monuments extolling the pax
      abound.
Faintly at first then thundering

came
The ponied eastern Riders.

39

Losing you today
Has extinguished all my life
With nothing now left.

40

Night and falling snow cast their shawls
        loosely about her
        standing classically
In the frail light of the single street lamp
        near Dammtor Station
        as the good Burger
Of Hamburg scurried past her with their bags
        of Wurste and cabbage
        and bottles of Bier,
And I am sorry I did not stop either.

41

God knows, you had no need to be
In Tulsa
        when America celebrated
        her two hundredth birthday.
You left your home to be with us that day.
We all said you looked awfully tired,
        but, oh Lordy, how you sang.
Thank you big Memphis man.

42

Your always smiling face was so clearly seen
        in the driving rain
On the train's platform we both knew so well
As you stood there watching me leave again
        without knowing when
        there would be a return
        to the other's wanting embrace.
So often we have spoken about and dreamed of
An end to this seemingly forever circle
        where there would be
        a place we could know
        would be there for us
        for all our tomorrows.

43

We had so many
Happy times in our long life
And now you are gone.

44

If you wander through those waterless regions
        looking aimlessly for rest
And unable to find what you believe you need
        as you walk
        as you run
        as you stumble
        as you fall,
Hope is needed to open your doors wide to full living.

45

Everything has been settled according
                         to common agreement
                         and is so noted.
Now,
If you will sign here,
                         your divorce
                         will be
Completed.

46

The old grandfather slowly pouring
       the fragrant green tea
       did not know
       in August
That the Manhattan Project
Would remove him from
       his wife
       his daughter
       his home.

47

There died a rose too soon
       growing by my door
       greeting only me
Each day in peace and beauty.
Who lived more: the rose or I?

48

What happened that day
To me, single, now with child?
What will Joseph say?

49

I am so afraid to tell you what I guess
      you must already
      know with terror
That I have only a few weeks left before
I must leave you forever.
This sorrow overwhelms me with constant
Thoughts of leaving you so very alone.
How can we be so separated after being
      together for so long?
There can never be any preparation for this
Endness which must visit all; yet we had
Always believed that we might escape
      the coming of a
      permanent night
Hoping in vain for forever days.

50

Hold me as I leave
As you did when we first met
That wonderful day.

51

There you stood, dear friend, that morning
      in the cold rain
      waiting
As you had done for years for those
Who chose you.

I had heard the end would come at six a.m.,
Long before you saw another English morning
      that January.
Though you stand patiently, I know you
Sense this place
      and would give
      more than your heart
      to be out on the route
Pulling the wagon laden with milk bottles
      one more time.
Do not look for me here. I could not
Bear your recognition.

God, how can your huge feet be so stilled
At this miserable seven a.m. foggy hour?

52

Preparations for a Bedouin wedding seem
      more exuberant
      than might be
      necessary, but life is too
Difficult there to be somber when two
Are to be joined.
And so it was that hot day in the desert
      that songs were sung,
      meat roasted, milk drank,
      and shots were fired.
But as the proud groom approached

    on his prancing horse,
    a bullet fired
    in joy
Sped through his body as his bride watched.

53

Those far thoughts of you haunt me always
Even as they find me running toward your
    lovely memory
    of vivid embraces
And plans for tomorrows full of each other.
I have no way to escape the constancy of those demons
Who pursue me through all boundaries everywhere
    until I am exhausted
    with the efforts
    to move without
    thoughts of you.

54

Wanting one more glimpse
Before you left me that day
Was my only hope.

55

When ravages of inevitable time have
    finally weakened me
And I can no longer hold you as when
    you first captured me;
And when even remembering the hope
Our life together gave us

       has faded
       from my memory;
I will somehow understand at that end
       that you will
       still be with me
Knowing that you told me long ago
You would carry me
       when
I could not walk
       on my own.

56

No Demerol here
Only the pain of real Birth
In a dirty barn.

57

Why is it that time for me now flies
      so softly,
And I know it has left me only when
I reach for today and find it already gone?
Somewhere in another room of the universe
My flown day flashes its color and
      then continues
      itself elsewhere
Leaving empty chairs ringed about with white
Ghosts both of laughter and crying.

If there ever is a new place made for me,
I will search for those ghosts of my flown days
And spend with each a thousand years so that
      I may finally
      know them
Because I never once knew them here.

58

The auction flyer said there were items
Too numerous to mention in addition
      to all those listed.
I guess that's right. How would
Memories of a sick baby with no
Money for a doctor be mentioned?
Or the elation of a son's high school

Diploma, the first in the family?
When the old house is finally emptied
        and all the buyers
        and the auctioneer
        have left,
I think there will still be items
Too numerous to mention.

59

Leaving you again
Must be similar to death
Since I am dying.

60

How has it come to this moment
        of parting
When we had always been together
Through so many problems of life?
I wish with all I am that I could
        rewind time
So that we were together again as before.

61

I never knew that it could be like,
But now I understand far too well
        what it is
        like to be
Hit with hard knowledge of an ending kind
And to be brought to my old knees
By a raw and visceral truth telling me
        that my only love
        is gone forever.

62

Hungry for time with too much of the past
    enslaving what little is left
    and knowing the weary arrivals
Of hope still-born
In too many letters,
What is the direction from whom is all
    one can ask.
More than far hills and glistening
    waters of foreign shores
    have to be secured before they
    come for me
    sitting here
Praying that once again some savior
Can revive what I gave too generously
Over the long years
    when giving was all
    I had
And no one remembered tomorrows.

63

This moment is not
What either of us had thought
Would ever happen.

64

I saw your last precious smile you gave me
    this evening
    of great sorrow
In that sterile room where you did not want
    to spend your
    remaining days.

What I would give if only I could reverse
Time to our earlier days of endless laughter
When each day was one of joy not despair.

65

The censors in the hot, dusty, fly-infested
Post office
    brusquely scissored open
    that late February afternoon
    the Christmas package
    mailed almost three months ago
By an anxious mother to her far away son.
The men in the little room
Kept
The two hometown weekly newspapers
Because they were printed in a western language
And charged an import duty
    on the mother's
    sugar cookies
After their examination showed nothing subversive
Was intended.

66

I know you told me often with care
That I should not go with them on the trip
So far away from you and our home
Where love and safety have constantly been.
I did not listen to your good words then,
    and now I
    wish I had.
They were in hindsight not the best of companions
Only because they had little regard for the laws
Of that beautiful but distant land of intrigue
Where what they thought was correct behavior
    was not acceptable;
    and now we find
    far too late
    we are guilty.

67

Never sweet sorrow
Is this cold final farewell
To all we once had.

68

The fog of lostness descends so starkingly quickly
      and wraps
        the left one
In shards of immediate and wholly insistent pain
While time goes wobbly as though there can never be
      any more time.
The one who remains forgets about everything
Outside the horrible ache which does not leave
As the world seemingly is unconcerned about
      the gaping hole
        placed in the lonely one.

69

The ambulance wailing
Past the sweating tired workers
With another statistic
Was heard by all of us driving
With the exception of Mr. Moore
Who, having the green light,
Drove his old Dodge pickup
Into the intersection
Into the ambulance.

70

My eyes, now so very strained

                    in their cages,
Strike against a darkened mirror
To find my way to you; and they
Must soon cease this effort
Or I will be blind.

71

We have found now at our final parting
The sustaining strength of our pervading love
Which long ago captured us so completely
    that without it
        no possibility existed
For our continued and full support of the other.
We know at this lonely moment of no more
That what we had at our beginning
Remains strong at our ending.

72

Wanting to see you
And knowing I now cannot
Burdens me fully.

73

Where have our questions gone which
        seemed to linger
In our learning and younger years
    as we searched
    for answers
    we thought
    the other had
For Hope beyond all our todays?

74

As I leave you now
Remember our lovely times
And not my going.

75

Brackish morning stole the last morsel
      she gave me
Before leaving with one suitcase and no
      farewells
      yesterday, I think; but yesterday
They said I was drunk again and
Reciting Goethe.
Sometimes being drunk and hearing inside
      my heart
      the Marienbad Elegie
Is like warm afternoon rains
      erasing her fragrance
      from my lonely bed.

76

We prayed fervently that what we heard this
      hard morning
Would never come to be in our life together;
But we heard even though the words sounded
      a finality
To everything we have wanted and loved
As we went through our only given time.

As I now descend slowly into my personal sunset,
      and while I can;
I hope with all the strength I have left

That you, my only love, will see a sunrise
        each day
And tell me that until I can no longer understand.

77

The strength we now have
Comes from our life of knowing
That the other was there.

78

Only the long sighs of beat men,
    not the moans of lovers,
    could be heard there
Carried by the restless winds
    under those blanching skies
Where hope lies in a molten river of promises
    like sunken angels' eyes.
And where yellowed pages burn once again dimly
    through the night
    and on into dawn
    while around the fire
    old men sing ancient words
For the young men, for the dying men
    who listen impatiently
To those incessant sounds promising much
    but giving little;
As camels grunt and women weep
Under the palms in the sands near the sea.

79

Finding our way together as we face
    our end
Will never be easy for either of us,
But we know fully and without doubt
That the other will be the source of strength
    we need

When that bleakest of times comes to us.

80

Some said what you did was an accident
And could never have been premeditated
    because you were
    a pillar
In this community just east of the Colorado River.
I was only passing through but decided
To stop
That morning the PTA member and husband
    of one wife
Shot
    his one wife
And then botched his shot to the head.

81

I saw you almost as though you were
    just beyond
    my grasp
As we met that first time of full wonderment
When neither knew the other.
I felt then a soft despair of not being
Able to see you again even as I hoped
    with my heart
    to remain with you.
Leaving you with my vivid memories
Of our walks during days and nights
Created a hunger I had never known
    before meeting
    you that day.

82

Holding now those thoughts

Of all our good yesterdays
Makes our end easy.

83

I am certain I saw it again last evening
>   moving along a star lighted pool;
>   so lonely appeared this dimmed figure,
>   this wisp of damask by the water's edge
>   that I knew it must have been my heart.

Alone with no hand to touch or voice to hear
>   moved that small part of me;
>   as I, remembering other evenings,
>   went on without pause though
>   hoping this could have been different.

84

Late London streets and uncertain steps cannot
>   be enjoyable
Say some nocturnal critics;
But let those be led as I was
>   by a haunting dark-eyed jewel
>   with dancing smiles,
And they will know as I do well
The sadness of no more late London streets.

85

Waiting in this desolately empty room
To be informed that the life of my life
>   is no more
Becomes so quickly a suffocating hard moment.
How can it be possible that the vibrant person
I knew so well no longer can be with me?
I comprehend well the ending of most things,
But this finality I am unable to grasp

today or ever.

86

The truly unthinkable has arrived far too quickly
      for us
Who thought it could never happen at any time
      to us.
This brutal ending of our life together should
Have waited beyond our knowing of each;
It has come without preparation of any kind
And without any feeling for what we mean
      to each.

87

Please do not leave me
Alone here without your smile
As a fallen leaf.

88

Beyond the wall they stood silent; the Russians
      said nothing
As the East German Volkspolizei questioned me.
And though I had come to Karl Marx Allee
      with nothing
But my umbrella to keep December snows
      from my barely covered body
And a small briefcase filled not with secrets
      but with chicken grease stained underwear
      (my Pension had no towels)
      and a Reader's Digest which they kept,
The people's police of the freedom loving socialist state
      for a moment
      made me see
      much more than

The Volksmuseum with its lovely Pergamon altar.

89

Too many say it is much easier for them
        never to Hope
That the mishaps they encounter in their lives
        can be overcome
        with prayer
        with belief
        with action
As they attempt to live only on their own.

90

You remain in my sight as though
        we had just met
With your dancing dark eyes fixed
        on me
Who had never seen such beauty.
There can be no recovery from this,
And today you have become an eternal spring
        for me.

91

Where have we forgotten our shared memories
        of times together
        spent in joy;
How should we remember as though from a faraway
Land of joined homes and dreams of those matters
Which make us whole though separate?

Who did this thing so long beyond all reaches
        of our memories
        of our wishes;
Who blinded us with mystique and incense

And lethal temple bells sounding so hollow
That all are now buried in elaborate tapestries?

92

To find you again
Is my only desire now
As I search each day.

93

Thelma, you bore his son and daughter
        before Iwo Jima
        tried to take him
        from you;
But he returned, and you died too young.

Ruth, you loved his son and daughter
        though they both
        were nephew and niece
        to you;
And he married you, but you also died too young.

Hazel, you bore his other two sons
        after the first children
        were grown and gone
        from him;
Now he has died too young, and what will you do?

94

Leaving my dear love
Can be compared to saying
This world has ended.

95

The old cathedral square in the city was filled
      with silent
      milling crowds
Held back from the center by armed young
      soldiers,
      some weeping,
Where two long black handkerchiefs tied
      around the heads
      of two hanging men
Flapped in the salty breeze from the harbor.

96

When your soul had been unhappily filled
      with grief
Which seems to reside without leaving you
      as you were
      as you desire
      as you plan
      as you pray,
Hope becomes the only solace you can fully trust.

97

The strength we now have
Comes from our life of knowing
That the other was there.

98

As you held me for one last time
Wanting both my pain to leave
And my life to remain,
I heard so clearly your whisper
That there was nothing you ever
Regretted during our many years together.
Hearing that from my only love
        was the reason
        I briefly hugged
        you tightly
        as before.

99

Our apartness must soon come to a
        fully realized
        end;
Or else we will find ourselves bereft
Even of those dreams which now sustain us.
Let us find a way, the way, any way
So that we may once again be together.

100

I reckon dreams die kind of slow
When a man is down and out
And can't get no work anywhere.

        Not since World War II
        Has such a high percentage
        Of American people been employed.

But maybe I'm not as bad off

As I think. I met a young man
The other day who hadn't been able
To get a job in more than a year.

    More jobs must be made
    Available to those who have
    Been bypassed until now.

I have to get on home now.
My wife will want to know
How I did today making the rounds
Just looking for work, any work.

101

Who forgot to tell you and me the meaning
      of black
In the cosmic color scheme of life?
Who wanted to cast you and me from each
Writhing out of our lovely paradise?
Why are those passive fabrications now
      made known
To us who wanted only to be together always?

102

Leaves now far too brilliant;
Brashly gay they became;
    fly softly
    slowly down
And seem to float on the face of life
Feeding in a lost unconscious memory.

103

Though we are now old and weak,
We still without effort daily
      seek
      find
      know
Our hopes of yesterday when we were young
As we rejoice in our dreams made real.

104

Our memories are not disturbed by our older days
      or by any matter
      which approaches us
      seen or even unseen
As we hold each other more strongly than ever before
Fending off all moments of every weakness
      before we are caught
      by that hard web
      spun by shortened days.

105

Though you cannot hear me this dark day
      in spite of
      my deepest wish,
I know somehow you realize I am still
      with the one
      of my early dreams.
Seeing you so frail is a moment I did not
      want to come
      in our life;
It is now here moving us as nothing ever
Before in our happy decades of being together.

I am here as I have always been
      with you
      only you.

106

Knowing you are there
Comforts me each time I think
  cannot go on.

107

When young morning masks revelers sad
       from long service paid to false loves
       during a night of eager eyes
       and glittering guides of servants

Who charmed with empty words spun from
       smooth mouths to entangle
       soft ears of guilty innocents
       in search of assurances,

What must remain for the secular and sacred
       garbage of easily discarded
       wrinkled minds and rent lives
       but tomorrow's surly collectors?

108

Do you remember when we were young
       and very much
       in love
And thought nothing could ever change
What we had in those long ago days?
Now that your end will too soon arrive,
We both still know firmly without doubts
That we remain to this ending moment
       very much
       in love.

109

When we pray that we will be mercifully spared
       from life's trials,
And in our asking believe that we will be

    delivered from evil
    protected from harm
    kept from wrong choices
    lifted from joylessness;
It is then that we must invite Hope into our lives.

110

He told me later after you had gone,
I hope you don't mind
    that I asked the man,
What I had guessed anyway in the lobby
As I sat watching you and trying
    not to watch you
Look at the door, then the big wall clock,
Then the door, then the big wall clock
While the minutes
Dragged.
Bus terminals are not the best places
    to be
    when you are
    lonely
And hoping that someone once loved
Will come
Through the door
And stop the big wall clock
    before the windowed hound
    leaves.

111

The simple, sleepy stable held more
    that cold night
Than tired oxen chewing their cuds
    in the dim light.
The penniless father, frightened by fate,

Moved as one possessed
    by unseen powers.
The teen-aged mother hoped her
Parents might be present
    as she
Presented the world her annunciated
    Counselor.

112

What vision is here
Holding us with our sad tears
Urging us today?

113

In the mountains of mankind's discontent
Bold rocks squeeze from the earth
    a drop
    and then another
    of grief
And hand them down with ragged hands
To fill the lower pool of sorrow where
    all wait
    with longings
    for the other.

114

We must have the strongest of wills
    for one more breath
    for one more prayer
    for one more day

Saving us from relentless remorse of our creating
And finding a way to be kind and loving
    to the only one
    who matters
In our unsatisfied lives we find ourselves.

115

How I wish I could walk
    once again
    across the streets
    hoping for a glimpse of your shining hair.

How I joyed in seeing you.
You, the one of the always smile.

Now the days are long
And the nights longer;
I walk out as before
    across the streets
    unknowingly hoping for a glimpse
    of your shining hair,

But you are gone.

116

I am well aware as I know you are,
    my life's love,
That I simply cannot make it on my own.
So take my worn hand and hold it tightly,
    my life's love,
And I will fight against my closing days.

117

Though we wish and pray with all our might
That our remaining time could slow down
      for us,
And though we know and understand so well
That this physically is impossible for all people;
We yet want more time together before there is
      no time left
      for us.

118

How I deeply wish
I could have just a few more
Hours with my darling.

119

There can never be a preparation for this coming
      of the lowest
      depths for man
When he is confronted by the flood of events
Which harvest the one left with no regard
For the suffering showered on the lonely one.
These terrifying consequences of having lived
      are hellish
      and abysmal
And can never be avoided by one of the two
Who pledged togetherness until death separates.

120

Were those the days we dreamed of
      and thought could never be
      when first we saw one another
In a strange land difficult for both?

Or were the few days only for
      our later dreams made easier
      by soft words not deeded
Which could never be forged by either?

Or did those days ever exist except
      in our late opened eyes
      moved by longings daring
For a moment to be understood?

121

This is not what we
Ever could have dreamed happen

To our happy life.

122

When words mean far less than intended
        and spoken hastily
To the one who should never have heard them
        in the morning
        in the afternoon
        in the evening
        or any time,
Each must remember that Hope always leads.

123

Hearing your familiar voice this early morning
        from the other side
        of this small planet
Wishing me a lovely day on my birthday
And telling me how much you wanted to be
        with me
        but cannot
Caused my heart to stumble and rejoice
        at the same time.

124

The mosque in the village was still echoing
        from the morning's
        call to prayer,
And the old men were shuffling toward the door
        to seek Allah
        and His blessing,
And the women were talking as they walked
        to the well
        for their water,
And the children were running around the camels

    to awaken
     the sleepy beasts;
When the thunder of strafing jets raced over them.

125

Far away are you
And my only thoughts of you
Are to be closer.

126

Why do we now ask as though we
      did not know
Where our joy for each has gone?
Is it better that we need to ask
If we somehow somewhere have
      abandoned this joy
      which once filled
      our lives
With moments we thought would never
      end?
Or is it far better to ask each boldly
How do we find again what we
      have lost
      through neglect
As we moved too easily in our lives
      together?

127

As we now begin this our final journey
      together as always,
We know we will face obstacles never before
Encountered on our beautiful journeys of the past.
We still see in the other the young and desired
      person of long ago
When our life stretched beyond all our horizons
Of plans, dreams, hope, and all we wanted.

Now our horizons are limited and at hand,
And all we can do is rejoice that we had
      those wonderful
        years together.

128

How I deeply wish
We were together again
As we once had been.

129

Hope gave us the strength to remain
      strong and faithful
When we were forced apart by matters
      not our choosing
      not our desire
      not our prayer
      not our belief,
So that we could comfort each other in need.

130

I try to imagine what you are feeling
      this desolate morning,
And I am unable ever to understand fully
What you must be thinking even as I am
      humbled by your love.
We are now on a journey which can have
      no good ending
For us who have survived treacherous times
Together as we painted our picture of a life

of strength and faith.

131

The headlines tonight did not tell it all
    or else
The readers would not have read only
    not guilty
    by insanity.
The wife and daughter will never read
In the headlines anytime the remaining truth:
    murdered man
    not replaced
    by insanity
Or sanity or not guilty or guilty or anything.

132

When we feel forgotten by the one we love
And ask where love could possibly be
In the midst of all the pain we know;
And as we struggle with our depths of uncertainty,
We can find in ourselves the strength
    which enables us
To understand that this harsh emotion
Must also be only a momentary step
On our journey of living fully.

133

We are faced with ardent and terse language
    telling you and me
    what we already knew
Spoken by those who believe profoundly that
This end news must be told immediately
    without kind preamble
So that everyone concerned may now be involved.

We tell each other when we are finally alone that
A broken spirit is more harmful than a broken body;
We say this not only because it is true
But also because we face this end now with courage
    from our love
      of many decades.

134

Stay with me just now
Even though we each fully know
You cannot remain.

135

We do understand with loving knowledge
That an end will come to all we have
    in each other.
We approach this finality with the same strength
We had in our earlier years when we freely gave
    to each other
What the other needed without prompting.
Though the end of our life together is unthinkable,
We will still be able to give to the other what
    each will need.

136

As lovers sail through those turbulent and deep seas
    of doubt and despair
Without being able to see any firm shores
    to rescue them
    to relieve them
    to comfort them
    to guide them,

They must always remember Hope will give them wisdom.

137

I never did learn your name and none
      of the seven with me knew either,
      but we can never forget
You.
We thought the little meadow with a few trees
      a hundred meters or so from the Grenze
      was perfect for a picnic
      that afternoon of the tenth of May
      when you came running, screaming,
      jumping, sliding, falling toward us
      and so suddenly, too burstingly quick
They shot you and dragged you back.

138

Are we living our lives in ways that
      always encourage others;
Or do we find that obstacles seem like
Mountains where our faith becomes too small?
Let us remind ourselves that failure can be a
      humbling experience;
And that each effort we sincerely make teaches us
When times are hard that failure is also a
      great life experience.

139

Now in our precious twilight always together,
We ask in vain how did our yesterdays go
      too quickly
      too soon?
Our arms which once held each other
So strongly have become burdened with time

And can no longer enfold the other as before.
Memories made from truly glorious moments
Are what now give us strength and hope
      for a few
        more days.

140

The joy we have now in our older days
        remained with us
As we moved with love through our
        joined lives,
And today we are enfolded everywhere
With all that we first found
So many good years ago
        in our younger days.

141

Wise ones have said through the ages
That love between two must lead
      to a narrow gate
      of a timeless departure,
And that this moment of deep sorrow
Can be understood as another beginning
      for those two
      who have loved well.

142

When we must sit at our sunset's dawn
And attempt to remember names, places, and objects
      from our early days,
We must walk with courage toward the end

Remaining as close as we ever were.

In our mirror we shared all our good life
We will have seen our faces before;
And now we must not hide from exposure
Because we are walking a different shore
      in our later days.

143

Knowing you there
Comforts me each time I think
I cannot go on.

144

Now listen carefully to what I'm going
        to tell you,
Because with the circumstances of your arrest
        involving
        drunken driving
        and resisting arrest
After you ran the stop sign and killed
        the young girl,
You'll get eight to ten with parole
        after three
        if you
Plead
Guilty to the charge of negligent homicide.

145

When we refuse to surrender to those moments
        of suffering,
Our souls will be refreshed and strengthened
        to withstand pains
        to endure tests
        to overcome temptations
        to forgive wrongs
Only because Hope now resides and presides in us.

146

Our seasons bear always some wisdom with them
As they are a strangely blind accompaniment to our
    moods and fancies.
Those season of our lives will sing with us
Or strike an able dirge of warning for us.
But when seasons flee from us too quickly
    without warning
And when storms of living rage out of hand
And when lightning strikes where lightning never was
And when unnamed things hang heavy in the air;
We must beware because more than a change
    is coming.

147

In the shattered world of those who learned
That the one whom they had committed all
Is no longer the center of their mutual universe,
Comes the dreadful realization through this
    painful awareness
That there cannot be a bridge across this
    great abyss.
While we have boundless belief in ourselves;
We have in us the ability to doubt all
That once had been secure and filled with
    a future.
There is nothing moral about making a promise;
The moral part all must learn is in keeping it.

148

Remembering you
Offers both joy and loss

Since you are not here.

149

I still remember even now in my much
        diminished state
When we were so very young and looking
Forward to our life spread before us to all horizons.
Though now I know I have almost
        reached the end
        of my part
With the one who shared everything with me,
I will fight to be with her until I have no more
        to give her.

150

One thing we have asked in our life together,
And one thing we have sought as we lived in joy;
That our final days of being in union
        would be
        filled with
        simple grace
So that our journey would end as it began:
Moments overflowing with unspeakable happiness
As we wait for our welcome to another journey.

151

Facing this endness from which we cannot escape,
And knowing there can be no tomorrows with plans
        and hopes
Of being together enjoying another day of comfort;
We are richly grateful for all the times of our past
When we laughed and loved and cried as we found
Overflowing happiness in only being with one another.
Now we will soon no longer see or hear the other

as we had joyfully
for so many
blessed years.

152

Torrents of our tears
Simply cannot remove fear
Of our unknowns.

153

We are the lonely children
    of the endless nights.
We have wept great floods
For we have been forsaken
    by love
And cannot hope to find it.
We can remember only dimly
    the joys of love,
But now these nights of no end
Keep us captured here alone.
We who are here in this place
Have learned too well the bitter lesson;
Only it is far too late.

        July, 1977
        Bucharest, Romania
        words of a patient
        in an insane asylum

154

Denying windows painted with evening's hues
    which speak too loudly
    of other windows, other evenings,
I tread once again the distant ways
And find the searching just as before.

Coming here meant losing what most I
        paid too dearly for
        far too long ago
When night's eve spoke softly to me
And promised music too distant to hear.

Moving on to other days with nights now
        too short to know
        and gifts too few to count
Is all that remains for me here
Who dreams only of other windows, other evenings.

155

How can our end be twisted into a grimace
        of deep grief
        and hurting agony
As we see in this suffering something that
Forces our eyes to close to the scene?
We are able to find in the other that strength
        forged in love
        over many years
Which now gives us the calming grace needed
        to understand
        and accept
        our end.

156

Joseph, I am scared.
Mary, we are not alone.
Please tell me again.

157

Where have our lovely years together gone,
And why did those go far too quickly
      as we lived
      and learned
Not really knowing that time is a cruel enemy
      to all who
      love well?

Let us fight against these passing days now
As we once fought for our future long ago,
      and we will
      continue to live
      and learn.

158

The rain is falling in this evening's dim light
As your tears fell in last morning's bright light
      when we were
      told we would have
Precious few days left to be together
Because of my very advanced illness.

Please do not weep for me in these
Last few days while we are yet together
      as we have always
      been in our lovely life
As we went with hearts joined by an
Unspeakable love for each.

Let us rather find once again the joy
Of memories made when we were young
      and wanted only
      the very best

For the other as we began our life's journey
Hand in hand until we must be parted.

159

The following is a true story which happened
      recently
      again
Recently
Frequently
In a Republic where all are created equally.
Only the name is changed to protect the bewildered:
Let's review our next applicant's resume.
Roger J. Stanly, PhD, twenty-three years' university
Teaching experience, six books, nineteen peer-reviewed
Articles, twenty-eight book reviews, and
Caucasian.
Too bad.
If he were the Pope, we could not hire him
To teach theology (said the candid chairman)
Because
His ancestry is not on the quota list.

160

Running from fear of the vast unknowns
      surrounding us
Provides no answers for our questions
      of the future
      of the past
      of the present
      of any time
Until we invoke Hope to join us in our journeys.

161

Holding with renewed effort to what we had been
      just a short
      while ago
Will never be in vain as we strive together
To regain what had been given us so frequently.
Running where so many have gone before us
      is not
      our option
As we realize that without the other's presence
Each will become far less than whole.

162

Return now to me
Is all I can consider
In my loneliness.

163

I know you saw me yesterday as I
    forgot
    again
What I had wanted to do for you.
I know also that you understand how
I am leaving you slowly every day.
When my mind is clear from the fog,
I am able to see you and remember you
    as before.

164

Erike told me on my return
That if they had caught
    me
Taking photos of the snarling guard dogs
And buxom women with machine guns,
    I
Would still be somewhere east of Magdeburg
Explaining that I was just a tourist
On a trip to see some museums.

165

I saw you there barely breathing
With your beautiful face wracked with pain
In a sterile bed not yours and not mine.
The ghostly memories of other rooms and other beds
    in our shortened union
    cannot provide relief
    from the awful finality
    of all being so wrong.

166

When we are tested in any manner
        by life,
We can know most assuredly that our
        trials we face
        trust we lose
        grace we forget
        courage we need
Will appear if we allow Hope to be with us.

167

Stumbling with only memories to guide you through
        the desolate valleys
While viewing in the distance the peaks of what
        once had been,
Your heart will cry out for a renewal of lost
Desires so that there may be a chance
For your mind to find wisdom which you
        foolishly squandered
On meaningless moments of ignorant falsehoods.
This precious lesson will be given to you
But once with hard definitions which you
        must master.

168

Entering my room
Where I cannot ever leave
You gave me such hope.

169

On Interstate Eighty a few miles west of Omaha,
    there is a fence
    and an old barn
    out in a field
    with some trees
    around a shed
    and a wedding ring
    in some tall weeds
    along the highway.
I stopped to help because I saw the old couple
On their knees
In the heat
Beating the weeds
Looking for her ring
Which had slipped off her bony finger;
They told me as I also looked in vain.

170

It is so much more important for us
    as we
    near our end
    together
To be aware of where we have been and how
    we have always
    supported one another
    through the decades
Than entertaining those false words which
    never give anything
    but must
    take everything
Which two in love in old age have worked
    so hard for.

171

Wanting you to be
Here with me and not just there
Pierces my sad heart.

172

Holding time as closely as possible means
That hours will not somehow become years
With lost hopes and plans forever vanished
    without knowing
    what happened.
Time does become meaningless when we forget
That nothing can prevent the erosion of it.

When we have gone beyond wanting to use
Our moments with each other and have
    with no regard
    to any consequence
Rashly believed that there will always be time
To do what we desire,
We will abruptly discover
    we have failed
    in living.

173

The company is sorry, Mrs. Dawson,
    but we can pay death benefits
    only on accidental deaths,
    and our attorneys yesterday,
After considerable effort and research, I might add,
    have determined finally
    that the tornado
    which killed your husband

      at our processing plant
And completely destroyed our facilities, I might add,
      was not accidental.
We will be able very shortly, I might add,
      to refund fully
      to you and your children
      the nineteen dollars
      and twenty-seven cents
Which your husband paid the last two months
On his accidental death policy.

174

When those inevitable and trying moments
      come to us
Without warning or provocation in our lives
      with discomfort
      with loudness
      with accusations
      with lies
We must truly know that Hope will protect us.

175

We knew that our beginning must have
      an ending
Even though we willfully denied such a truth.
Many say we are completely inseparable
As we face the finality of our good life
      together.
We now have no understanding how lonely
The other will be facing life alone.
What we do understand and remember well
Is that we wait in our ending
For the other just as we once did
      in the beginning.

176

I understand that your older sister brought
You to my clinic,
      and that your father
      is no longer at home
      and that your mother
      worked at two jobs.
I believe the nurse has explained to you earlier

The legal and medical procedures.
Since you are only twelve,
    I must ask
    you and your mother
    to sign these forms
In the presence of a county legal aid attorney
Before I can abort
The fetus
Your older brother caused you to carry.

177

These last hard moments
Can never erase our thoughts
Of what went before.

178

Your embassy somehow managed to deny to all
Publicly and with frivolous detail
    that you simply
    were not here
    in London
    much less
    in a hospital
With twenty-six other mangled men.
But I saw you,
And you knew me that contorted evening
When you invoked for me the always calming
    peace be on you;
And then asked
About Alia, your wife of love and strength,
And Khalifa, your son of hope and joy,
    both
    so far

so far
　　　from you,
Ahmed, warrior of the desert and friend of mine.

　　　　　　179

Days run tripping and rippling
　　　like autumn grasshoppers,
　　　and though these times
　　　are meant to be loved;

There lies in you a hungry longing
　　　augment not soothed
　　　by the graceful fall of a leaf
　　　or by the touch of familiar hands.

While nights flee silvery and shimmering
　　　like morning rains
　　　embracing the begging earth
　　　with ever-returning life,

There flay within too many desperations
　　　born perhaps in younger
　　　autumns of brash decisions
　　　when songs seemed clear.

　　　　　　180

The tired mother of eight sons and five daughters
　　　sat heavily in the shade
　　　of a giant oak tree
　　　wiping the running sweat
　　　from her bronzed face
　　　with a tattered rag
As she watched some of her children play

Near the big wild blackberry patch
Thick with flitting insects and humid ripeness.
I better pick some more she said.
My Will loves my cobblers,
And he will come home from the sawmill
All worn out;
    and my blackberry cobbler
    will help him
    forget tomorrow
    for awhile
    tonight.

181

How is it possible that this hard time
    has come
When I must utter those heavy words
    of a forever goodbye
And know that none of my tomorrows can never
    be the same
Without the beautiful girl of all my springs
Or the lovely woman of my endless summers
Being with me so full of life and laughter?

182

I

What was it like, son of Albuquerque,
    that afternoon
    among the rubber trees
    somewhere near Pleiku
When you lay on a grenade meant for others?

II

Mr. and Mrs. Diego Alvarado?
                       Yes.
I am Army Specialist Fourth Class Johnson.
                       Yes?
I regret
                       No! No!
That the Department of Defense
                       Please hold me.
Has asked me
                       Dear, dear God.
To inform you
                       Help me.
Of the death
                       Oh, Jesus, Jesus!
Of your son,
                       Ramon, Ramon!
Ramon.
                       No, please, no!

III

We award this Congressional Medal of Honor
        I remember his first grin
To your son who displayed courageous action
        and his first day of school
Far beyond the call of duty on the battlefield
        and his first girl friend
In total disregard for his personal safety
        and his first old car
Posthumously.
        and his last goodbye.

IV

Go to sleep.

Go to sleep.

May the good Lord

Your soul

Safely keep.

Go to sleep.

Go to sleep.

You gave

For us

Your life,

Ramon

Now you have

For all eternity

The peace of Arlington.

Made in the USA
Columbia, SC
30 December 2017